The Senses

SMELL

Angela Royston

Chrysalis Children's Books

First published in the UK in 2005 by
Chrysalis Children's Books
An imprint of Chrysalis Books Group Plc,
The Chrysalis Building, Bramley Road,
London W10 6SP

ISBN 1 84458 168 3

British Library Cataloguing in Publication Data
for this book is available from the British Library.

Editorial Manager: Joyce Bentley
Senior Editor: Rasha Elsaeed
Editorial Assistant: Camilla Lloyd

Produced by Bender Richardson White
Project Editor: Lionel Bender
Designer: Ben White
Production: Kim Richardson
Picture Researcher: Cathy Stastny
Cover Make-up: Mike Pilley, Radius

Printed in China

10 9 8 7 6 5 4 3 2 1

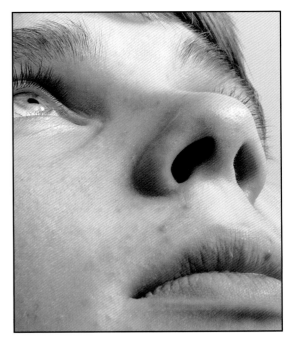

Words in bold can be found in New words on page 31.

Typography *Natascha Frensch*
Read Regular, Read Smallcaps and Read Space; European Community Design Registration 2003
and Copyright © Natascha Frensch 2001-2004 Read Medium, **Read Black** and *Read Slanted*
Copyright © Natascha Frensch 2003-2004

READ™ is a revolutionary new typeface that will enchance children's understanding through clear, easily
recognisable character shapes. With its evenly spaced and carefully designed characters, READ™ will help
children at all stages to improve their literacy skills, and is ideal for young readers, reluctant readers and
especially children with dyslexia.

Picture credits
Cover: Bubbles/Loisjoy Thurstun. **Inside:** Bubbles: pages 4 (Lucy Tizard), 6 (Sarah Vivian Prescot), 9 (Loisjoy Thurstun),
10 (Loisjoy Thurstun), 11 (David Robinson), 13 (Claire Paxton), 14 (Loisjoy Thurstun), 17 (Chris Rout), 19 (Loisjoy Thurstun),
20 (Ian West), 23 (Frans Rombout), 24 (Frans Rombout), 25 (Ian West), 27 (Ian West), 28 (Angela Hampton), 29 (Loisjoy
Thurstun). Corbis Images Inc.: pages 15 (Joel Stettenheim), 21 (Corbis Royalty-free), 26 (Nick Hawkes/Ecoscene). Steve
Gorton: pages 1, 2, 5, 7, 8. 12, 16, 18, 22.

Contents

What is smell?

Smell is the **sense** that tells you about **scents**, **odours** and **fumes** in the air around you.

Your nose and brain work together to give you your sense of smell.

Into your nose

When you breathe in, air goes through your **nostrils**.

Inside your nose are many tiny **nerve endings**. These detect smells in the air.

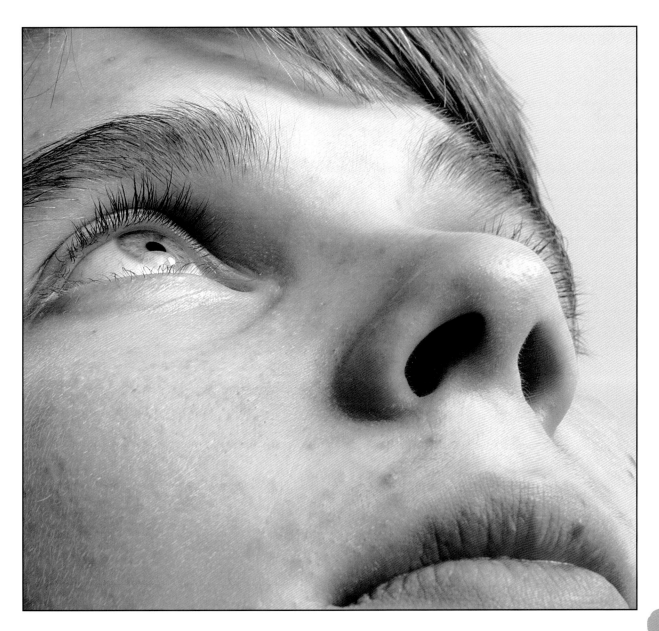

Floating in air

Something smells when **particles** of it float in the air that you breathe.

You smell a flower when some of its particles go into your nose.

Sweet smells

Perfume smells sweet. Most people like sweet smells.

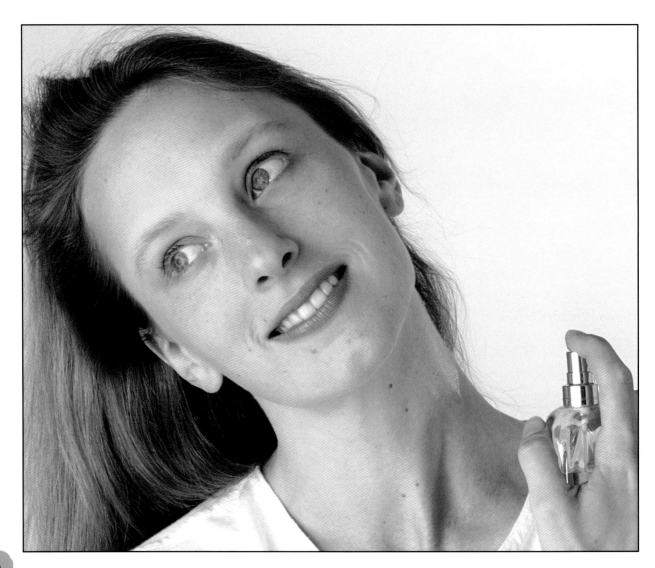

In a food market, the sweet smells of fruit fill the air.

Fresh smells

Green leaves and grasses smell fresh and clean.

Mint smells very fresh, too. Most toothpastes smell of mint.

Strong smells

Strong smells are easy to **recognise**. Cut up onions and garlic smell very strong.

Tarmac, the black material used to cover roads, also has a strong smell.

Cooking smells

Cooked food smells such as fried fish, tomato soup and roast chicken are easy to recognise.

Newly baked biscuits smell so good you want to eat them straight away.

Nasty smells

Rotten food smells nasty. This warns you not to eat it.

Sweaty socks and shoes can smell really horrible!

Outdoor smells

At the seaside, the smells of seaweed, salt water and sand fill the air.

Factory chimneys release smells high in the air. Wind blows the smells far and wide.

Smell and taste

Your senses of smell and taste are similar. These cheeses smell and taste very strong.

The smell of food cooked on
a barbecue can make you
feel hungry.

Memories

Babies recognise their mother because they remember how she smells.

The smell of a farm reminds you of other farms and zoos you have visited.

Danger!

The smell of smoke warns you that something is burning.

The smell of a cigarette is strong and not very pleasant.

Smelling well

You cannot smell when you have a cold and your nose is blocked. But it will soon clear.

Look after your nose and sense of smell! Blow your nose gently to get rid of **mucus**.

Quiz

1 How does air get inside your nose?

2 What makes something smell?

3 What does perfume smell like?

4 What kind of smell does toothpaste have?

5 Which smells are easiest to recognise?

6 Why does rotten food smell nasty?

7 How does a baby recognise its mother?

8 What happens when you have a cold?

The answers are all in this book!

New words

fumes smelly pollution in the air, such as car exhausts and factory smoke.

mint a herb with a strong, fresh taste and smell.

mucus thick liquid made inside your body.

nerve endings parts of the body that react to particular things, such as smells.

nostril opening into your nose.

odour natural, bad smells, for example sweaty feet, unwashed clothes and rotten food.

particle a tiny part of any solid, liquid or gas that is too small to see.

perfume something that people put on their skin to make them smell nice.

recognise know what something is.

scents natural, pleasant smells such as those from flowers.

sense the way you find out about your surroundings. You have five senses – sight, hearing, smell, taste and touch.

sweaty full of sweat from a person's body.

Index